The World of Color

White in My World

by Joanne Winne

Children's Press
A Division of Grolier Publishing
New York • London • Hong Kong • Sydney
Danbury, Connecticut

Photo Credits: Cover and all photos by Thaddeus Harden
Contributing Editors: Mark Beyer and Magdalena Alagna
Book Design: Michael DeLisio

Visit Children's Press on the Internet at:
http://publishing.grolier.com

Library of Congress Cataloging-in-Publication Data

Winne, Joanne.
    White in my world / by Joanne Winne.
      p. cm. — (The world of color)
    Includes bibliographical references and index.
    Summary: A simple story highlights such white things as vanilla ice cream, a white cat,
clouds, and milk.
    ISBN 0-516-23127-8 (lib. bdg.) — ISBN 0-516-23052-2 (pbk.)
    1. White—Juvenile literature. [1. White. 2. Color.] I. Title.

QC495.5.W567 2000
535.6—dc21

                                                                                    00-024366

Contents

My name is Cathy.

I like to play outside.

What do you see outside that is white?

My **daisies** and **tea set** are white.

The **clouds** and the chairs are white, too.

7

I feed my cat in the **kitchen**.

I pour her milk into a bowl.

What do you see in the kitchen that is white?

9

The cat is white.

The milk and the bowl are white, too.

11

I have lunch.

I have a **sandwich**.

Can you count how many foods are white?

12

13

There are two white foods.

The bread is white.

The cheese is white, too.

15

Then I have **dessert**.

Do you know what this white ice cream is called?

17

This ice cream is called **vanilla**.

Vanilla ice cream is white.

You can eat it with a red **cherry** on top!

19

White can be found everywhere.

What do you see around you that is white?

21

New Words

clouds (**clowdz**) puffy white things floating in
  the sky

daisies (**day**-zeez) a type of white flower

dessert (deh-**zert**) the sweet food you eat at
  the end of a meal

cherry (**cher**-ee) small, red fruit that is sweet

kitchen (**kich**-in) room in a house where the
  cooking is done

sandwich (**sand**-wich) a food made of some-
  thing between two slices of bread

tea set (**tee set**) cups and a tea pot that are
  toys

vanilla (vuh-**nil**-luh) a flavor of ice cream

To Find Out More

Books
Little White Dog
by Laura Godwin and Dan Yaccarino
Disney Press

Hunting the White Cow
by Orchard Books
by Tres Seymour and Wendy Anderson Halperin

Web Site
Crayola
http://www.crayola.com
This is the official Crayola Web site. It contains lots of pictures to print and color, as well as craft activities, games, and online art.

Index

About the Author
Joanne Winne taught fourth grade for nine years. She currently writes and edits books for children. She lives in Hoboken, New Jersey.

Reading Consultants
Kris Flynn, Coordinator, Small School District Literacy, The San Diego County Office of Education

Shelly Forys, Certified Reading Recovery Specialist, W.J. Zahnow Elementary School, Waterloo, IL

Peggy McNamara, Professor, Bank Street College of Education, Reading and Literacy Program